CGP has Year 4 Spelling practice covered!

The best way for pupils to improve their Spelling in Year 4 (ages 8-9) is by doing as much practice as they can.

That's where this book comes in. It's packed with questions that'll test them on all the crucial Spelling skills, including those introduced for the first time in Year 4.

And there's more! Everything is perfectly matched to the National Curriculum and we've included answers at the back. Enjoy!

What CGP is all about

Our sole aim here at CGP is to produce the highest quality books — carefully written, immaculately presented and dangerously close to being funny.

Then we work our socks off to get them out to you — at the cheapest possible prices.

Published by CGP

Editors
Keith Blackhall, Heather Cowley, Catherine Heygate, Gabrielle Richardson, Hayley Shaw, Sam Summers
With thanks to Andy Cashmore for the proofreading.
With thanks to Laura Jakubowski for the copyright research.

ISBN: 978 1 78294 128 6

Clipart from Corel®
Printed by Elanders Ltd, Newcastle upon Tyne.
Based on the classic CGP style created by Richard Parsons.

Text, design, layout and original illustrations © Coordination Group Publications Ltd. (CGP) 2022
All rights reserved.

Photocopying this book is not permitted, even if you have a CLA licence.
Extra copies are available from CGP with next day delivery • 0800 1712 712 • www.cgpbooks.co.uk

Contents

Section 1 – Prefixes

Prefixes — 'dis' and 'mis' 4
Prefixes — 'in', 'il', 'im' and 'ir' 6
Prefixes — 're', 'anti' and 'auto' 8
Prefixes — 'sub', 'super' and 'inter' 10

Section 2 – Suffixes and Word Endings

Suffixes — Double Letters 12
Suffixes — 'ation' and 'ous' 14
Suffixes — 'ly' 16
Word Endings — 'sure' and 'ture' 18
Word Endings — The 'shun' Sound 20
Word Endings — 'gue' and 'que' 22

Section 3 – Confusing Words

Word Families 23
The Short 'i' Sound 24
The Short 'u' Sound 25
The Hard 'c' Sound 26
The Soft 'c' Sound 27
The 'sh' Sound 28
The 'ay' Sound 29
Plurals and Apostrophes 30
Homophones 32

Spelling Hints and Tips 35
Answers 36

Section 1 — Prefixes

Prefixes – 'dis' and 'mis'

A **prefix** is a letter or group of letters that can be **added** to the **beginning** of a word to make a **new word**.

'dis-' is a **prefix**.   dis- ➕ honour ➡ **dis**honour

'honour' is the root word.

The prefixes '**dis-**' and '**mis-**' have **negative** meanings.

not allow ➡ **dis**allow   not behave ➡ **mis**behave

① Split the words below into prefixes and root words.

disorder ➡ *dis* ➕ *order*

mislead ➡ *mis* ➕ *lead*

disown ➡ *dis* ➕ *own*

② Draw lines from the prefixes to the correct root words.

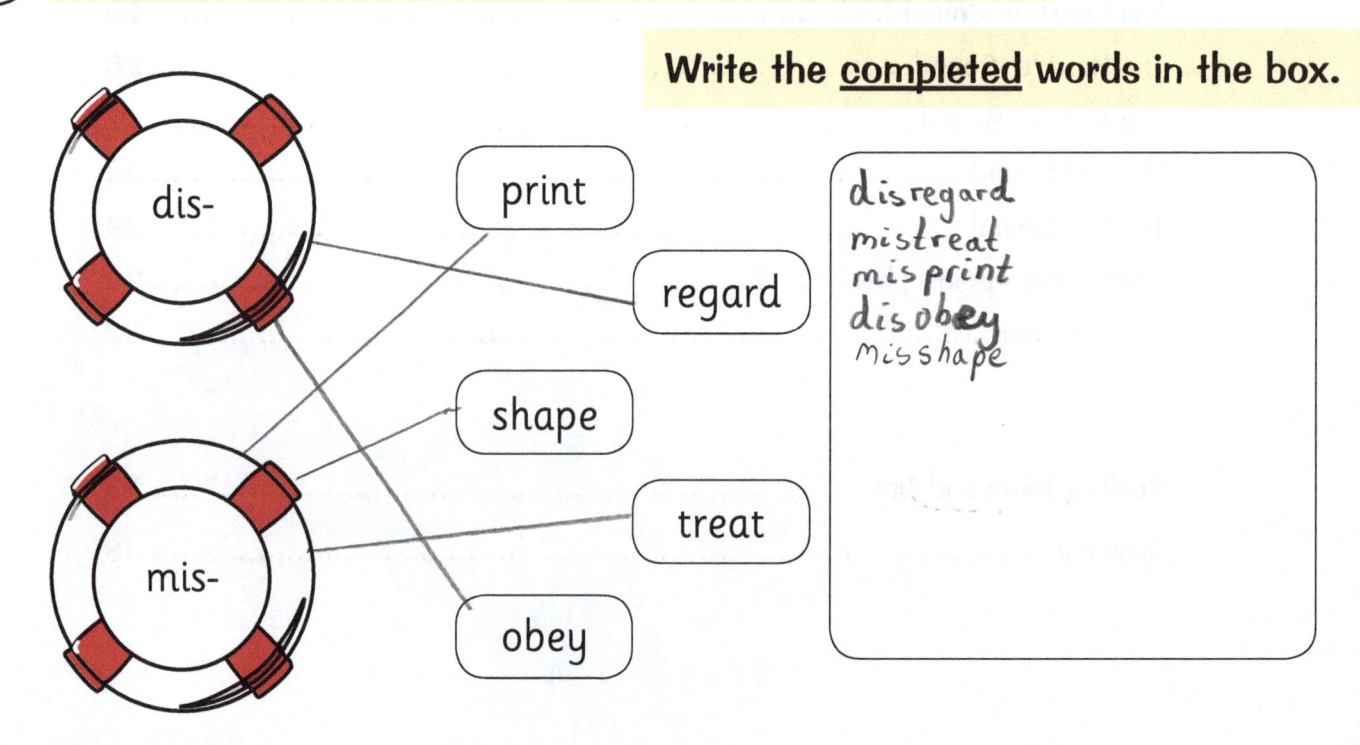

Write the **completed** words in the box.

- dis- → regard, obey
- mis- → print, shape, treat

disregard
mistreat
misprint
disobey
misshape

3) Complete the words in these sentences using dis- or mis-.

The ....dis.... advantage of living in Britain is that it rains a lot.

The thief stared at the policeman in ....dis.... belief.

When I ....mis.... hear what's said, it's easy to ....mis.... understand.

Jun says he has £1000 in the bank, but he's ....mis.... calculated.

We had to ....dis.... connect our telephone line to install a new one.

When Dina had a tooth out, she ....mis.... pronounced lots of words.

Tim was ....dis.... appointed to find that Sam was ....dis.... honest.

4) Add dis- or mis- to each word so it matches the description.

to tell someone the wrong information → ....mis.... inform

to judge something incorrectly → ....mis.... judge

to spell something incorrectly → ....mis.... spell

to vanish → ....dis.... appear

to not agree → ....dis.... agree

5) Use the letters and the clues to spell words beginning with dis- or mis-.

to use something incorrectly — misuse

to not like something — dislike

Now Try This: Use a dictionary to find three words starting with 'dis-' or 'mis-' that you haven't seen before. Write a short paragraph that includes all three words.

Section 1 — Prefixes

Prefixes – 'in', 'il', 'im' and 'ir'

The prefix 'in-' means 'not' when you add it to a root word.

inefficient ← 'inefficient' means 'not efficient'.

The prefix 'in-' sometimes changes to 'il-', 'im-' or 'ir-'.

illiterate   immobile   irremovable

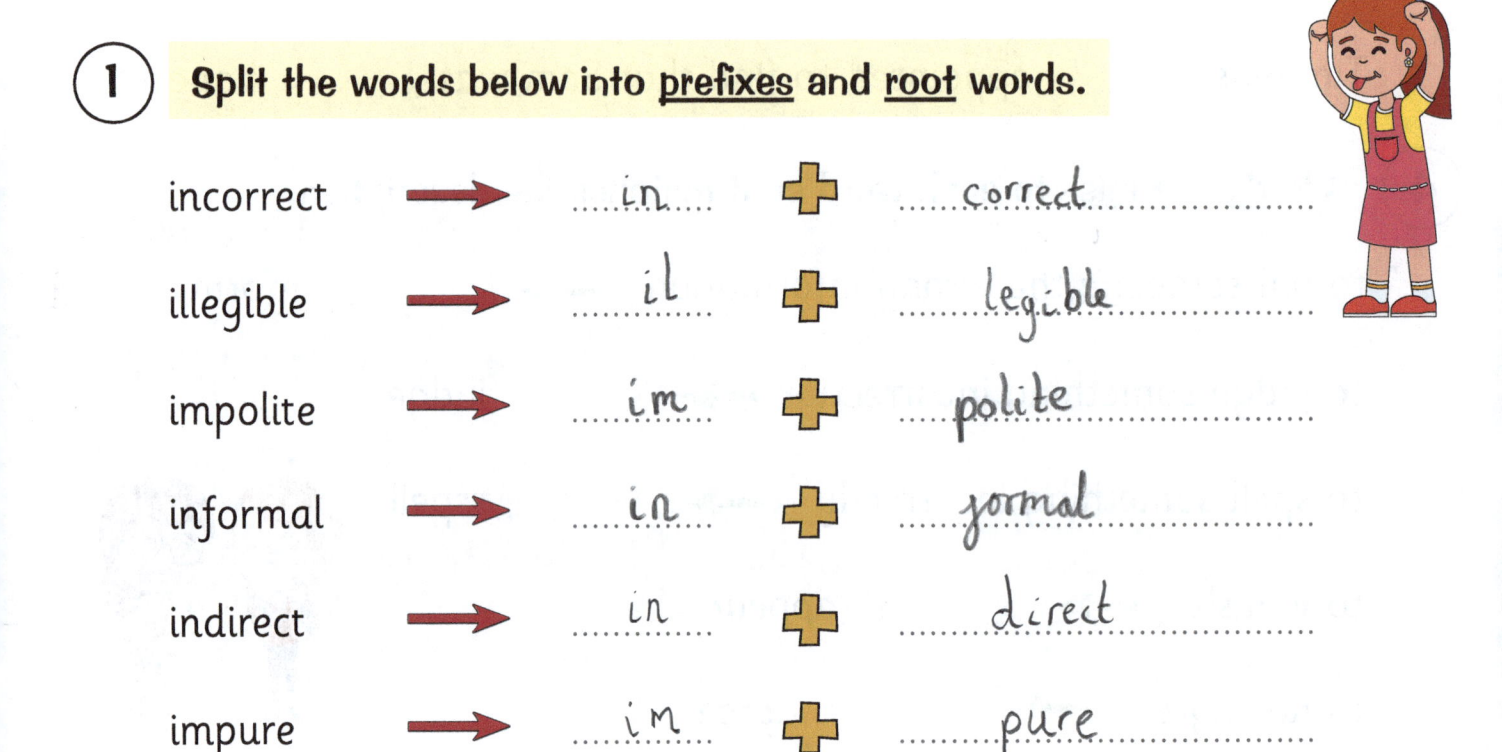

1) Split the words below into prefixes and root words.

incorrect → in + correct
illegible → il + legible
impolite   → im + polite
informal   → in + formal
indirect   → in + direct
impure   → im + pure

2) Circle the correct spelling of each word to complete the sentences.

Fantasy characters who can't die are inmortal / (immortal).

Gemma thought the remark was imoffensive / (inoffensive).

Colin had to scrap his car because it was (irreparable) / ilreparable.

The tools they supplied were simply inadequate / (iradequate).

Section 1 — Prefixes

3 Use the clues to write a word beginning with in-, il-, im- or ir-.

not capable → *incapable*

not possible → *impossible*

not rational → *ilrational*

not logical → *inlogical*

4 Draw lines from the prefixes to the correct root words.

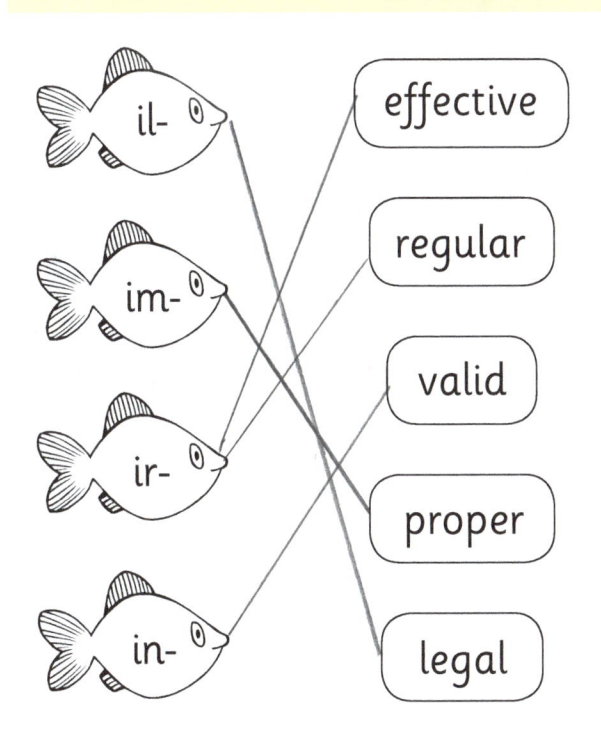

il- — effective
im- — regular
ir- — valid
in- — proper
    — legal

Write the completed words in the box.

illegal
invalid
irregular
ireffective
improper

5 Complete the words in these sentences using in-, il-, im- or ir-.

Olivia kept hurrying me along — she's so *in*patient.

Rahim's account of what happened was very *in*accurate.

I think chocolate, cake and biscuits are *ir*resistible.

The story made no sense — it was completely *il*logical.

We can't trust Jason with anything — he's very *ir*responsible.

Now Try This Pick three words from the box in question 4 and use each one in a sentence.

Section 1 — Prefixes

Prefixes – 're', 'anti' and 'auto'

The prefix 're-' means 'again' or 'back' when you add it to a root word.

readjust ⟵ 'readjust' means 'to adjust again'

'anti' means 'not' or 'against' ⟶ antisocial

'auto' means 'self', 'own' or 'automatic' ⟶ autograph

1) Add re-, anti- or auto- to finish each word correctly.

...**anti**.climax   ...**re**.design   ...**auto**.pilot

...**anti**.biotic   ...**re**.appear   ...**re**.emerge

...**re**.open   ...**anti**.septic   ...**re**.fresh

2) Circle the correct spelling of each word to complete the sentences.

When I dance with Leo, we spin (anticlockwise) / reclockwise.

Pete has automarried / (remarried) — his new wife is called Kim.

When Elvis came to town, I asked for his antigraph / (autograph).

I need to (resend) / antisend my email to Rashida.

Yara needs some revirus / (antivirus) software for her computer.

Miss Hoffmann decided to (rephrase) / autophrase her comment.

Section 1 — Prefixes

3) Use the clues to work out each word starting in re-, anti- or auto-.

apply again → r e a p p l y

a u t o m o b i l e ← another word for 'car'

decorate again → r e d e c o r a t e

a n t i s o c i a l ← unsociable

arrange again → r e a r r a n g e

4) One word in each of the sentences below has the wrong prefix. Rewrite the sentences so that all the words are spelt correctly.

The correct spellings all start with re-, anti- or auto-.

Fred is writing his rebiography.

Fred is writing his autobiography.

I need to antido my homework because it got wet.

I need to redo my homework because it got wet.

Antiturn the form in the envelope provided.

Return the form in the envelope provided.

In winter, people use autofreeze spray on their cars.

In winter, people use antifreeze spray on their cars.

Mrs Potter antiheats her leftover meals in the microwave.

Mrs Potter reheats her leftover meals in the microwave.

Now Try This: In a book or magazine, try to find one word you don't know that has the prefix 're', one that has 'anti' and one that has 'auto'. Look up their meanings.

Section 1 — Prefixes

Prefixes – 'sub', 'super' and 'inter'

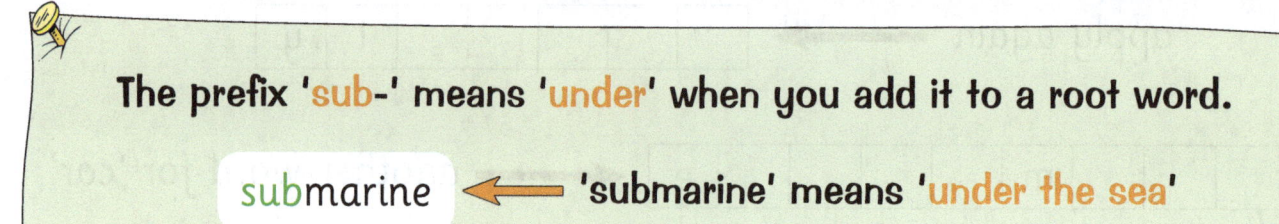

The prefix 'sub-' means 'under' when you add it to a root word.

submarine ← 'submarine' means 'under the sea'

'super' means 'above' or 'more than' → supersonic

'inter' means 'between' or 'among' → intermix

1) Circle the correct spelling of each word to complete the sentences.

Mick is looking to superlet / sublet his apartment.

Pam calculated the subtotal / intertotal to be £10.60.

Our school has run out of subglue / superglue.

2) Draw lines from the prefixes to the correct root words.

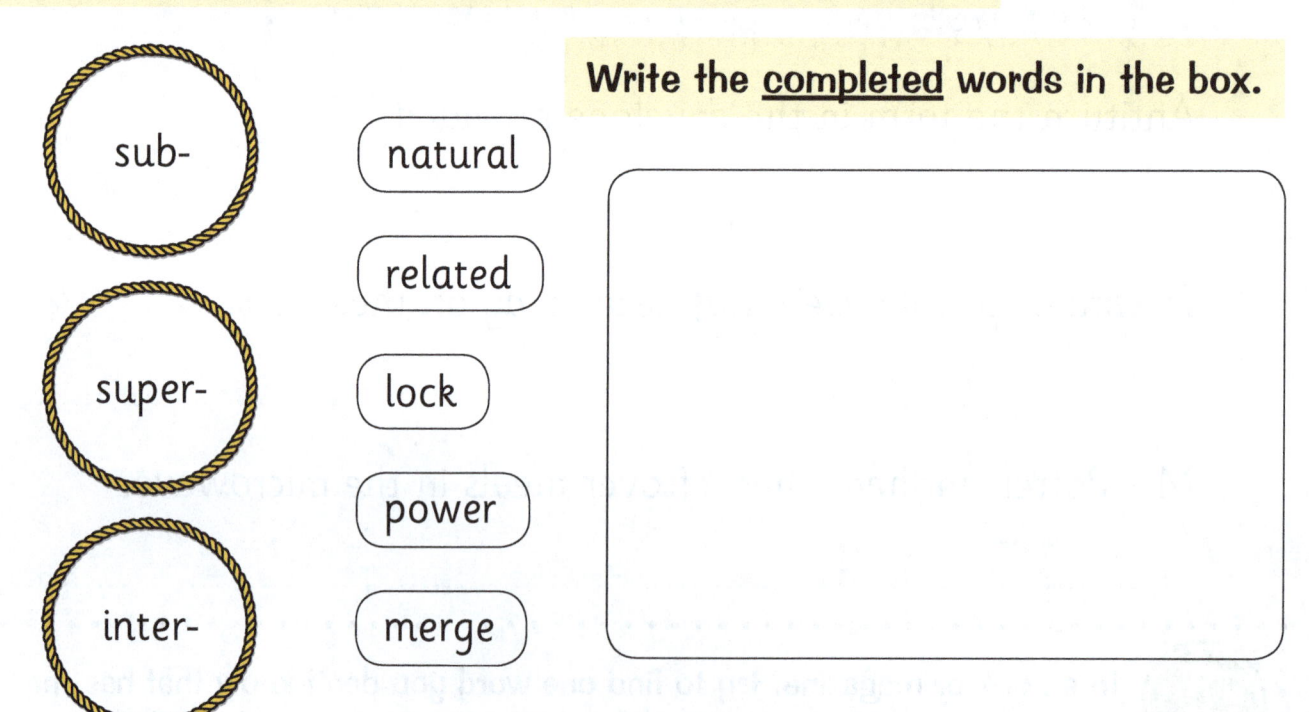

Write the completed words in the box.

- sub-
- super-
- inter-

- natural
- related
- lock
- power
- merge

Section 1 — Prefixes

3 Complete the words in these sentences using sub-, super- or inter-.

The best lessons at school are the .... active ones.

Akin met Mildred on an .... city train from York to Leeds.

.... headings can make instructions easier to follow.

If the picture falls off the wall, try using .... glue.

Ellie wants to be a .... star when she's older.

Nigel can lift a car — people say he's a .... man.

We .... divided our group's share of the work.

4 Use the clues to work out what each word is. Write the words in the boxes.

This can travel underwater. → [ ][ ][ ][m][ ][r][ ][ ][ ]

[ ][ ][ ][ ][ ][m][ ][ ][ ][ ][ ] ← You might do your shopping here.

5 Write a sentence using each of the following words.

subtitle

....

superhero

....

international

....

Now Try This Write a short paragraph about a child with magical powers. Use as many words starting with 'sub', 'super' and 'inter' as you can.

Section 1 — Prefixes

Section 2 — Suffixes and Word Endings

Suffixes – Double Letters

A **suffix** is a letter or group of letters that can be **added** to the **end** of a word to make a **new word**.

When you add a **suffix** to some words you have to **double** the last **letter**.

'forget' is the **root word**. → forget + -ing → forgetting

'-ing' is a **suffix**. The 't' is **doubled**.

1) Put a <u>tick</u> in the boxes next to the words that are spelt <u>correctly</u>. Put a <u>cross</u> in the boxes next to the words that are spelt <u>incorrectly</u>.

preferred ☐   offerring ☐   equipped ☐

prefered ☐   offering ☐   equiped ☐

2) Add the suffix <u>-ing</u> to the words below. Some words need double letters so that they are spelt correctly. Then write the <u>completed</u> words in the correct column in the table.

swim..............

run..............

jump..............

stop..............

play..............

garden..............

begin..............

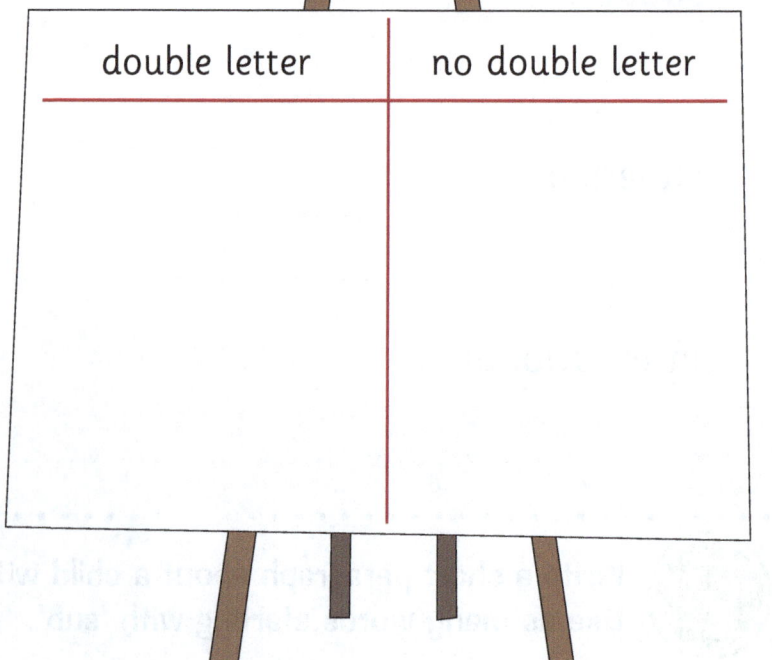

double letter	no double letter

3) Circle the correct spelling of each word to complete the sentences.

The trip to the zoo is limitted / limited to just ten people.

We were very annoyed when our flight was cancelled / canceled.

The polar bear jumpped / jumped off the iceberg and into the water.

Salma could hear the people singging / singing in the street.

4) Add the suffix -er to spell the words below correctly.

begin + -er → ....

garden + -er → ....

hot + -er → ....

swim + -er → ....

5) Circle the words spelt incorrectly in the passage below.

On holiday, Danny traveled to America and visitted New York. It was a great trip, but he regreted doing a bungee jump. His ears started poping and he began feelling very unwell when he looked down. He definitely won't be doing that again.

Write the correct spellings in the box.

Now Try This: Look through a few pages of a newspaper or magazine. Circle every '-ing' word containing a double letter, and then write down its root word.

Suffixes – 'ation' and 'ous'

For some words you don't need to change the spelling of the root word when you add the suffixes '-ation' and '-ous'.

peril + -ous → perilous

Sometimes the spelling of the root word changes when you add '-ation' or '-ous'.

The 'e' in 'sense' disappears.

sense + -ation → sensation

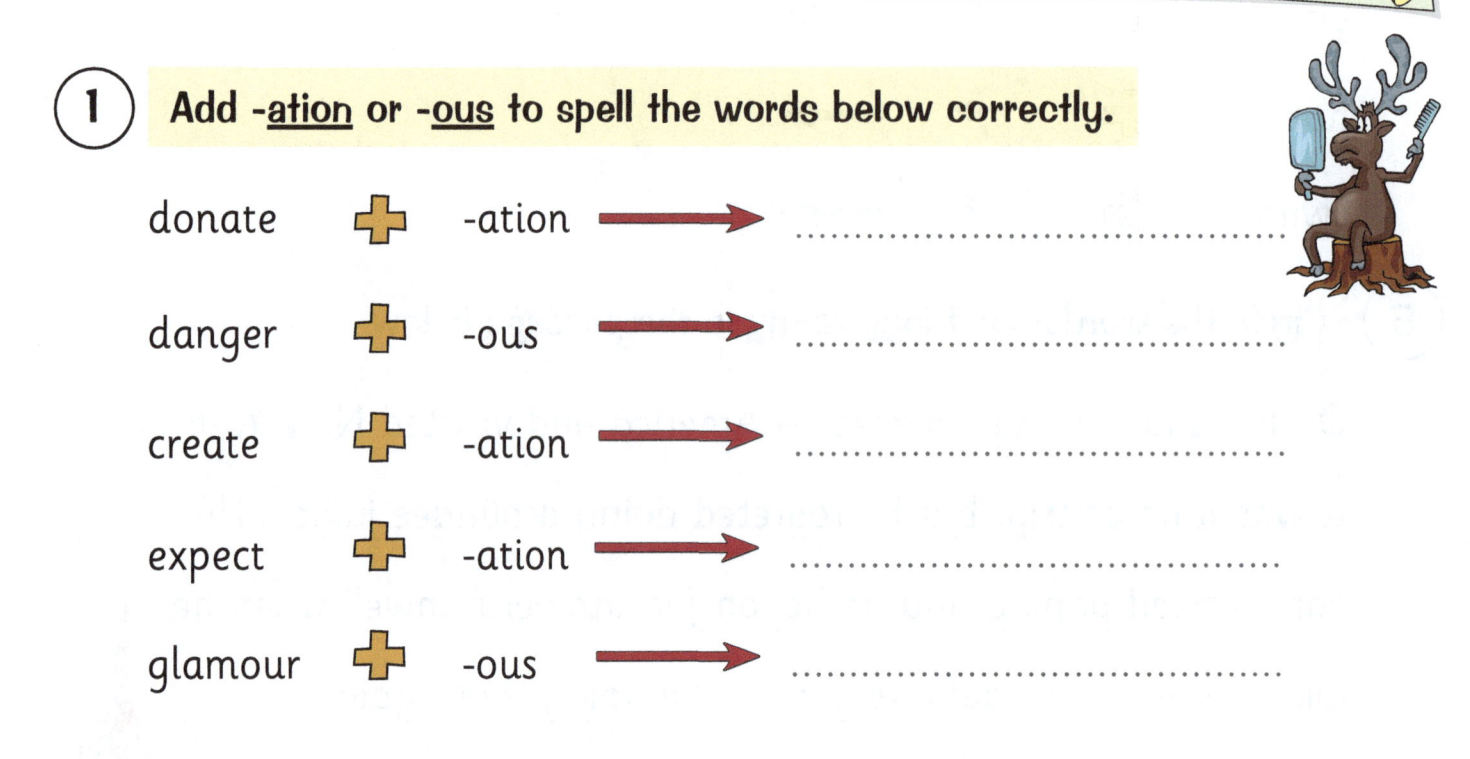

1 Add -ation or -ous to spell the words below correctly.

donate + -ation → ....

danger + -ous → ....

create + -ation → ....

expect + -ation → ....

glamour + -ous → ....

2 Underline the words below that are spelt incorrectly. Then write the correct spellings on the dotted lines.

limitation   humourous   ....

couragous   infestation   ....

hazardous   infectous   ....

senseation   ....

Section 2 — Suffixes and Word Endings

3) Add -ation or -ous to the sentences below so that they make sense.

A hot bath with calming music is a great form of relax............. .

Maria thought the cost of the holiday was outrage............. .

Travis asked for more inform............. about the trip to Portugal.

4) Use the clues to work out each word ending with -ous.

an area with lots of mountains is... → | | o | | | t | | i | | | |

| h | | m | | | | | | ← another word for 'funny'

some snakes are... → | | | i | s | | | | | |

5) Circle the words spelt incorrectly in the passage below.

In Croston, prepareations are under way for the summer celebrateions. Inviteations have been sent to lots of fameous people and an enormous amount of effort has been made to get this locatetion ready for the festival. Based on early indicatetions, the organisation in charge expects hundreds of visitors to come to Croston.

Write the correct spellings in the box.

Now Try This: Pick three words from page 14 ending in '-ation' and '-ous'. Use them to write a short dialogue between two characters.

Section 2 — Suffixes and Word Endings

Suffixes – 'ly'

For some words you don't need to change the spelling of the root word when you add the suffix '-ly'.

live + -ly → lively

Sometimes the spelling of the root word changes when you add '-ly'.

The 'e' in 'humble' disappears.

humble + -ly → humbly

1 <u>Rewrite</u> each word below with an **-ly** ending.

Remember — the spelling of some words changes when '-ly' is added.

sad → sadly

double → doubly   safe → safely

glad → gladly   quick → quickly

subtle → subtly   cuddle → cuddly

2 Find <u>seven</u> words ending in **-ly** in the wordsearch. Write these <u>words</u> on the dotted lines.

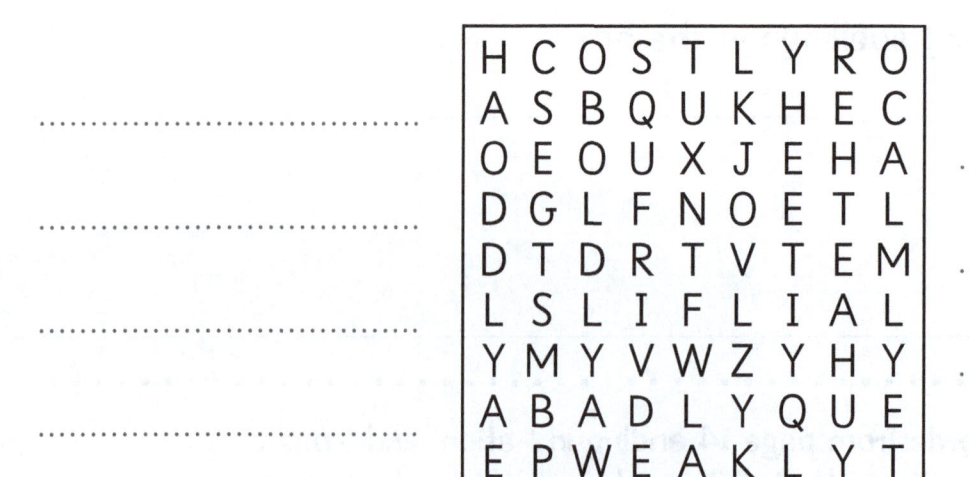

```
H C O S T L Y R O
A S B Q U K H E C
O E O U X J E H A
D G L F N O E T L
D T D R T V T E M
L S L I F L I A L
Y M Y V W Z Y H Y
A B A D L Y Q U E
E P W E A K L Y T
```

costly, badly, weakly, boldly, calmly, softly, oddly

Section 2 — Suffixes and Word Endings

3 Circle the correct spelling of each word to complete the sentences.

The three bears franticly / frantically searched for their honey.

Mr Miller was completely / completly surprised to see his sister.

Rosie gentlely / gently closed the door behind her.

Simba was truely / truly sorry for what he'd done.

Repairing the living room curtains was very fiddlely / fiddly.

The knight noblely / nobly walked up to the king.

4 Draw lines from the words in the columns to the correct words ending in -ly in the clouds.

simple

easy

angry

deadly   deadily
easyly   easily
angrly   angrily
busyly   busily
simpely simply
happly   happily

happy

dead

busy

5 Add -ly correctly to each of these word beginnings. Then write the word in a sentence.

comic................

....

final................

....

Now Try This Write two sentences, each one containing two words ending in '-ly'.

Section 2 — Suffixes and Word Endings

Word Endings – 'sure' and 'ture'

The endings '-sure' and '-ture' sound similar, but are spelt differently.

closure   capture

1 Draw lines from the word beginnings to the correct word endings.

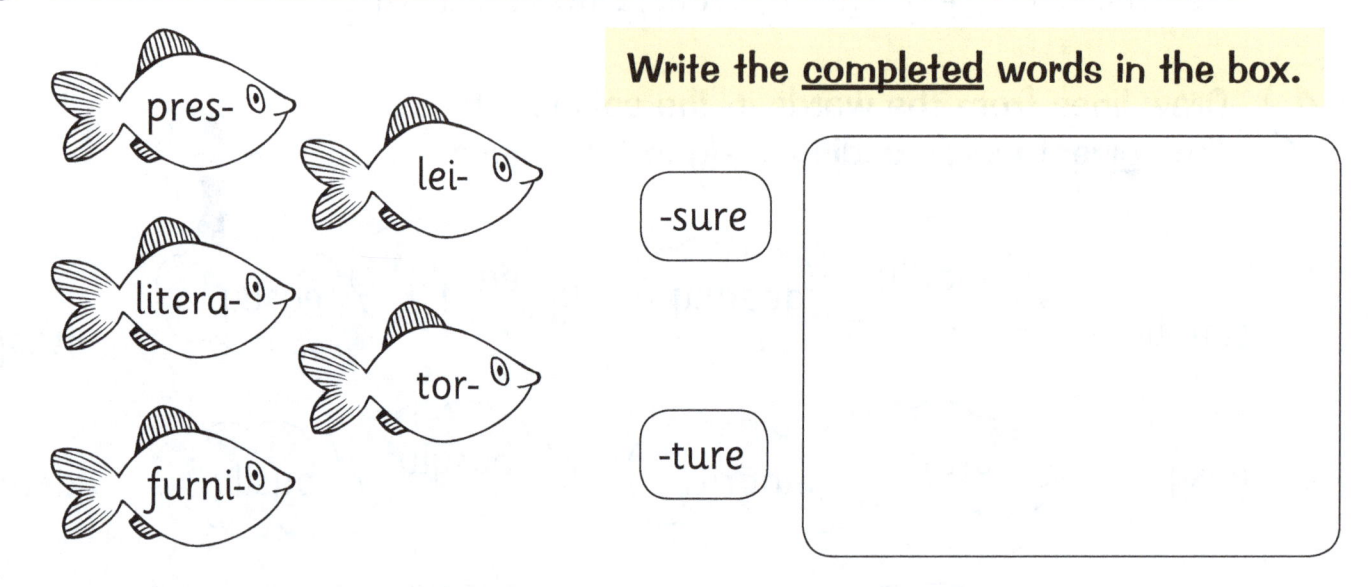

Fish: pres-, lei-, litera-, tor-, furni-

Write the completed words in the box.

-sure

-ture

2 Add -sure or -ture to spell the words below correctly.

enclo- + ... → ....

adven- + ... → ....

mix- + ... → ....

manufac- + ... → ....

expo- + ... → ....

compo- + ... → ....

ges- + ... → ....

Section 2 — Suffixes and Word Endings

3 Complete the table by filling in the missing words. All the words end in -sure or -ture.

Clue	Word
pirates look for this	t....................
you might hang one of these on your wall	p....................
you might keep an animal in this	enc....................
in winter, the t.... outside can drop below freezing	t....................
if you sign something, you put your s.... on it	s....................

4 Add -sure or -ture to spell the words in the passage below correctly.

After the heavy rain, Mr Pattinson decided to reas.................... his tenants that he would inspect the struc.................... of their house for signs of mois..................... If necessary, he would mea.................... the roof tiles and order some replacements. However, the recent clo.................... of his local DIY shop means that he will have to wait a while before he can place an order.

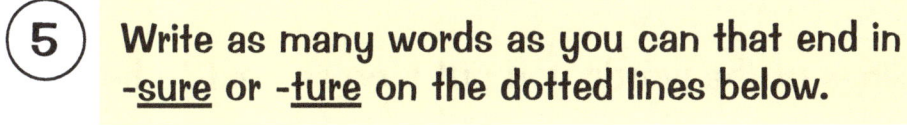

5 Write as many words as you can that end in -sure or -ture on the dotted lines below.

....

....

Now Try This — Write three sentences, each containing a word from question 5.

Section 2 — Suffixes and Word Endings

Word Endings – The 'shun' Sound

When it comes at the end of words, the 'shun' sound can be spelt in different ways.

Careful — there are some exceptions to these rules.

act ➡ ac**tion**

'-**tion**' is usually used when the root word ends in '**t**' or '**te**'.

tense ➡ ten**sion**

'-**sion**' is used when the root word ends in '**d**', '**de**' or '**se**'.

optic ➡ opti**cian**

'-**cian**' is used when the root word ends in '**c**' or '**cs**'.

express ➡ expre**ssion**

'-**ssion**' is used when the root word ends in '**ss**' or '**mit**'.

1) Put a tick in the boxes next to the words that are spelt correctly. Put a cross in the boxes next to the words that are spelt incorrectly.

polition ☐   complecian ☐   permission ☐

division ☐   attencian ☐   hesitacian ☐

musicsion ☐   mention ☐   confesion ☐

Write the correct spellings of the words you put a cross next to below.

Section 2 — Suffixes and Word Endings

2 Draw lines from the word <u>beginnings</u> to the correct word <u>endings</u>.

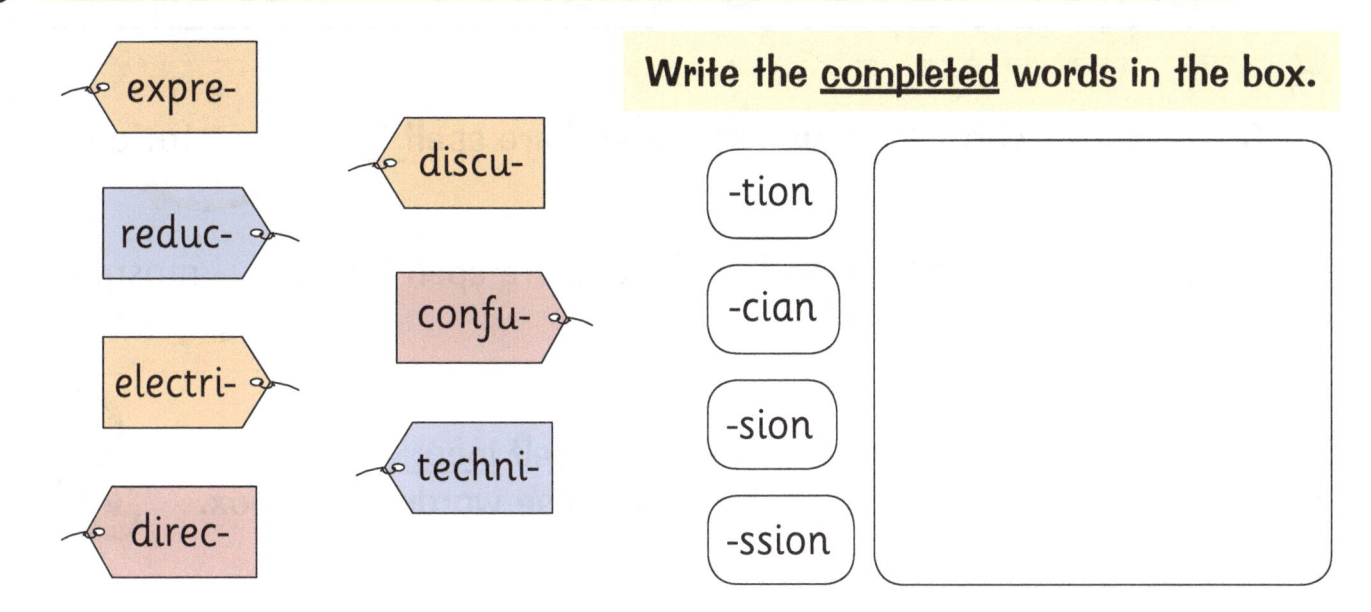

Write the <u>completed</u> words in the box.

- expre-
- discu-
- reduc-
- confu-
- electri-
- techni-
- direc-

Endings: -tion, -cian, -sion, -ssion

3 Solve the <u>clues</u> to complete the crossword.

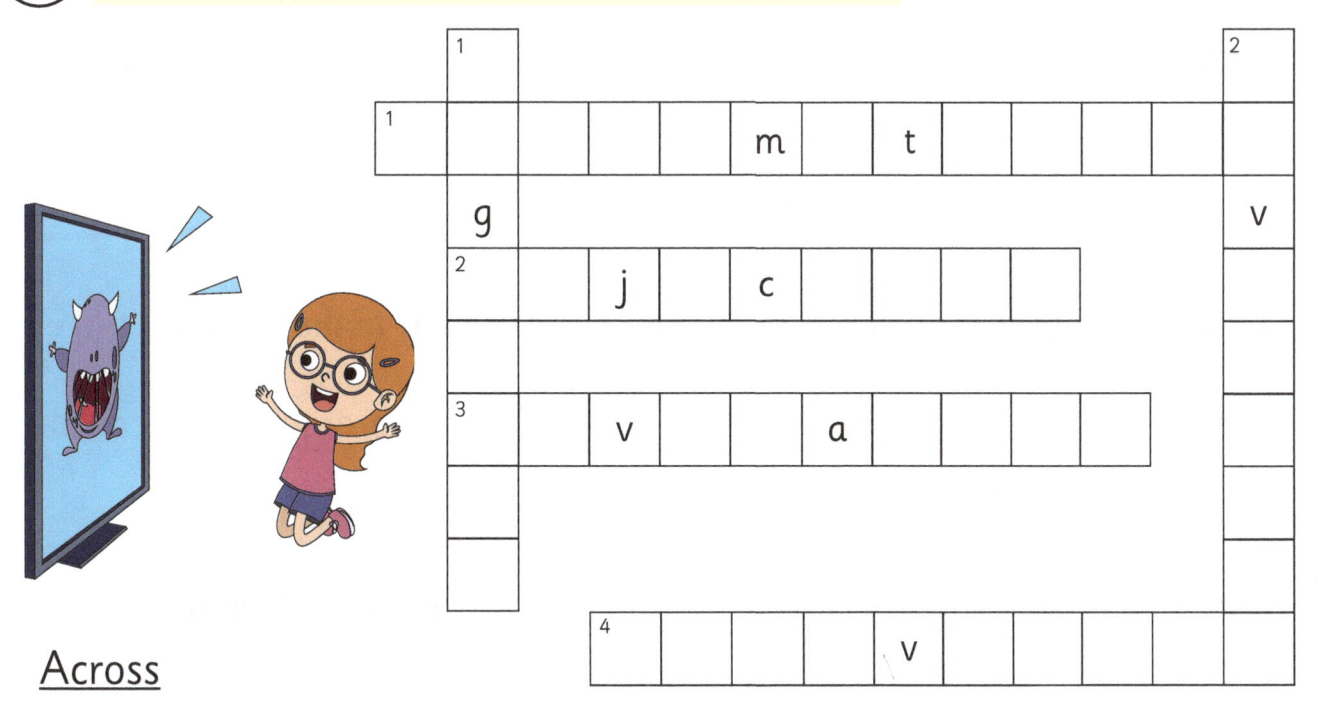

Across
1. This person is good at maths.
2. Another word for a 'jab'.
3. This invites someone to something.
4. You watch TV programmes on this.

Down
1. This person can do magic.
2. Inventors come up with this.

Now Try This — Write a short story about the two people who appear in the crossword answers.

Section 2 — Suffixes and Word Endings

Word Endings – 'gue' and 'que'

Some words with a 'g' sound at the end are spelt 'gue'. → fatigue

Some words with a 'k' sound at the end are spelt 'que'. → mosque

1 Underline the words below that are spelt incorrectly. Then write the correct spellings of these words in the box.

song catalog wrong

vague gong

dialog

league intrig

2 Add k or que to the sentences below so that they make sense.

Javed has an old, valuable anti............. from the eighteenth century.

The robbers left the ban............. with bundles of cash.

Ayako was pleased with the criti............. of her latest play.

I'm so thirsty — I really need a drin............. .

3 Write a sentence with a word ending in gue or que on the dotted lines.

....

....

Now Try This How many words ending in 'gue' and 'que' can you think of in two minutes?

Section 2 — Suffixes and Word Endings

Section 3 — Confusing Words

Word Families

Word families are groups of words that contain the same root. Their meanings are related — like a family.

user
reuse
useful

All of these words contain the root 'use'.

1) Tick the words below that are in the same word family as sport.

play ☐   sporty ☐   sorted ☐

athlete ☐   sportsmanship ☐   unsporting ☐

2) Add prefixes or suffixes to these words to make pairs of words that are in two different word families.

..............agree..............   ....play..............

..............agree..............   ....play..............

3) Write down a word that belongs to the same word family as each of the pairs of words below.

thoughtful   afterthought   ....

rewrite   songwriter   ....

discover   recovery   ....

Now Try This: Write down two groups of three words from word families not on this page.

Section 3 — Confusing Words

The Short 'i' Sound

The short 'i' sound can be spelt with an i or a y.

discover   mystery

1 Circle the words below that are spelt correctly.

knyt   Egypt   piramid   witch

myth   twyg   gym   dyscreet

2 Put a tick in the boxes next to the words that are spelt correctly.
Put a cross in the boxes next to the words that are spelt incorrectly.

sistem ☐   rapyd ☐   satisfy ☐

sympathy ☐   abolysh ☐   phisics ☐

Write the correct spellings of the words with a cross in the box below.

[ ]

3 Complete the sentences below using the correct words from the box.

mystakes / mistakes   symbols / simbols

This is very good work — there are only a few ....

Maps have lots of .... on them.

Now Try This — How many words with short 'i' sounds can you use in one short paragraph?

Section 3 — Confusing Words

The Short 'u' Sound

The short 'u' sound can be spelt in several different ways.

trouble   glove   uncle

1 Use the picture clues to correctly spell the short 'u' words below.

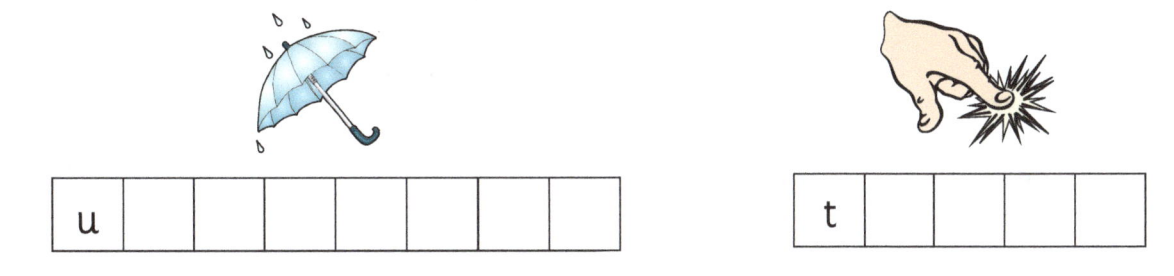

| u | | | | | | |

| t | | | | |

2 Complete the sentences using words with short 'u' sounds.

Two people can sleep in a d.............................. bed.

At least n.............................. was broken.

R.............................. means the opposite of smooth.

My br.............................. is much more annoying than my sister.

My aunt's daughter is my c.............................. .

3 Write each of these words in a sentence.

country ➔ ....

young ➔ ....

enough ➔ ....

Now Try This Write three sentences, each containing a word with the short 'u' sound.

Section 3 — Confusing Words

The Hard 'c' Sound

The hard 'c' sound is like a 'k' sound. It can be spelt several different ways.

sto**ck**   s**k**etch   pani**c**   s**ch**eme

1 Circle the words below that are spelt correctly.

classik   leak   ockupy   chord

brick   sckool   smoke   electric

2 Fill in the missing letters to complete each word correctly. All the words have a hard 'c' sound.

....aos   awa....e   ....emist   an....or   ....aracter

....ettle   tri....   ....are   e....o   sti....

3 Complete the sentences below using the correct words from the box.

socker / soccer   mekanic / mechanic
kalendar / calendar   chorus / corus

If your car breaks down you should call a ....

The .... of a song is repeated between verses.

A .... shows all the days in each month.

The American word for football is ....

Now Try This — Write a sentence about a day trip which uses two words with a hard 'c' sound.

Section 3 — Confusing Words

The Soft 'c' Sound

The soft 'c' sound is like an 's' sound. It can be spelt in different ways. → scissors   peace

1 Circle the words below that are spelt **correctly**.

| prinsess | offise | pace | consert |
| science | onsce | recipe | crescent |

2 Underline the words below that are spelt **incorrectly**. Then write the **correct** spellings of these words on the dotted lines.

prinsce   mice

parscel   deside   circle

decend   precise

sincere   recent

suspence

....
....
....
....
....

3 Write each of these words in a **sentence**.

discipline → ....

fascinate → ....

scent → ....

scene → ....

Now Try This — List the names of at least two types of transport that contain a soft 'c' sound.

Section 3 — Confusing Words

The 'sh' Sound

The 'sh' sound can be spelt in several different ways.

bishop   chalet   sugar

1) Fill in the missing letters to complete these 'sh' sound words.

wi........   poli........   ....arade   radi........

........ivalry   pres........ure   ....immer

........adow   para........ute

2) Complete the sentences using the 'sh' sound.

The ....ef cooked an amazing meal for us.

The bro........ure said there would be a buffet.

I'm ....ure I'm right about this.

The washing ma........ine has stopped working.

The pari........ church is just down the road.

3) Write each of these words in a sentence.

insure ➡ ....

punish ➡ ....

moustache ➡ ....

Now Try This — Give six words containing the 'sh' sound that you might hear in a shop.

Section 3 — Confusing Words

The 'ay' Sound

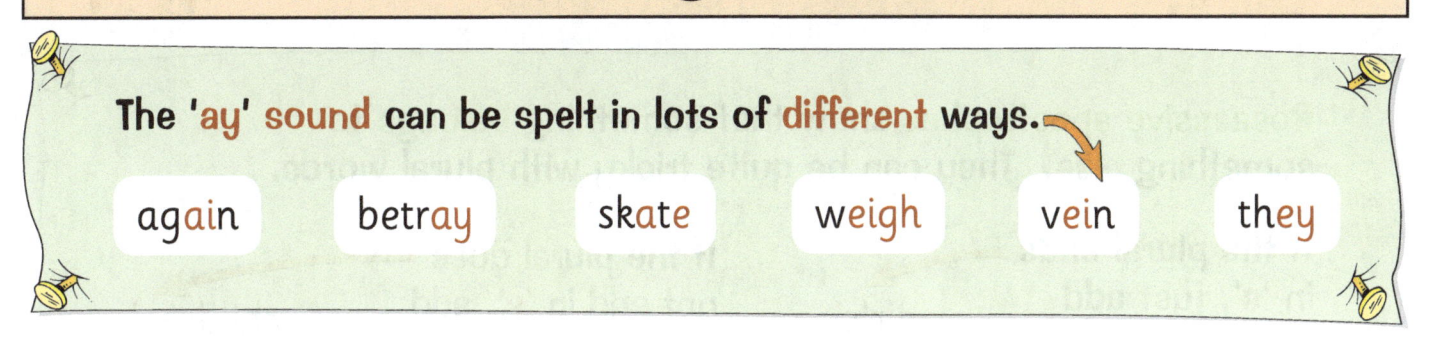

The 'ay' sound can be spelt in lots of different ways.

ag**ai**n   betr**ay**   sk**a**t**e**   w**eigh**   v**ei**n   th**ey**

1) Circle the words that are spelt incorrectly.
Write the correct spellings on the dotted lines below.

| obay | veighl | neibour | taste |
| rein | away | estimate | shaike |

....

2) Complete the sentences below using the correct words from the box.

freight / fraite   afrayed / afraid   hesiteite / hesitate

Emma is .... of spiders.

Trains are used to transport .... around the country.

I wouldn't .... to confront him.

3) Rearrange the letters below to spell a word with the 'ay' sound.

(p, a, l, i, n)   (e, h, g, i, t)

....

Now Try This: List four words with the 'ay' sound not found on this page.

Section 3 — Confusing Words

Plurals and Apostrophes

Possessive apostrophes show that something **belongs** to something else. They can be quite tricky with plural words.

If the plural ends in **'s'**, just add an **apostrophe** on the end. → girls'

If the plural does not end in **'s'**, add an **apostrophe** and an **'s'**. → children's

1) Tick the phrases which use apostrophes <u>correctly</u>.

The foxe's cubs ☐   The witches' cauldrons ☐

Everyones' favourite ☐   The women's handbags ☐

2) Below are some <u>plural words</u>. Write them out correctly with a <u>possessive apostrophe</u>.

men → ....   deer → ....

beaches → ....   cats → ....

3) <u>Underline</u> the phrases which use apostrophes <u>correctly</u>.

the elves hats / the elves' hats

the ladies' coats / the ladie's coats

the boxes' labels / the boxe's labels

the calves' mothers / the calve's mothers

the policemens' handcuffs / the policemen's handcuffs

the companies' employees / the companies employees

Section 3 — Confusing Words

4 **Rewrite** the phrases below using an **apostrophe**.

The footballs belonging to my brothers ➔ my brothers' footballs

The books belonging to the students ➔ ....

The toys belonging to the children ➔ ....

The scarves belonging to the snowmen ➔ ....

5 Draw lines to **match** the sentences which mean the **same** thing.

- More than one shoe belonging to more than one girl
- One shoe belonging to one girl
- One shoe belonging to more than one girl

- The girl's shoe
- The girls' shoe
- The girls' shoes

6 Write a **sentence** using a **possessive apostrophe** and the words below.

mice mother ....

snakes tongues ....

geese wings ....

Now Try This — Extend three of the correct phrases in question 3 into full sentences.

Section 3 — Confusing Words

Homophones

Homophones are words that **sound** the same, but have different **meanings** and **spellings**.

mail — Mail is another word for post.

male — A male is a man or boy.

1) Draw lines to match each word with its meaning.

piece
peace

- calm and quiet
- part of something
- simple or ordinary
- a flying vehicle

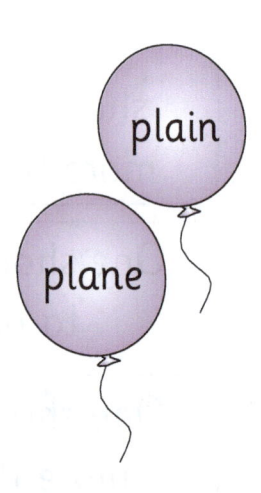

plain
plane

2) Circle the correct spelling of each word to complete the sentences.

It's very dangerous to leave your bags in the I'll / aisle / Isle.

The I'll / aisle / Isle of Wight is the largest of England's islands.

I'll / Aisle / Isle make sure I'm there to pick you up at four.

3) Circle the word that has been spelt incorrectly in each sentence. Then write the correct spelling on the dotted line.

I usually eat breakfast at ate o'clock. ....

The prince is the air to the throne. ....

Male dear have big antlers. ....

Section 3 — Confusing Words

4) Fill in the gaps in these sentences using the correct words from the box.

> he'll   heel   heal

.... definitely be late.

Shoes that don't fit properly often rub on the ....

I hope my injury will .... soon.

5) Find homophones for the words below.

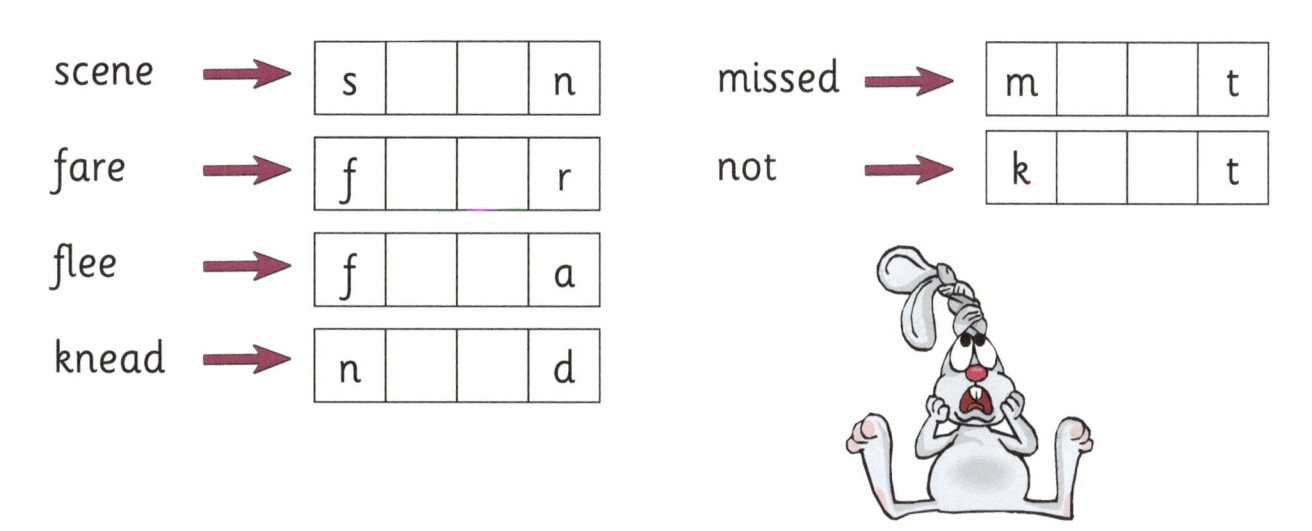

scene → | s | | n |

fare → | f | | r |

flee → | f | | a |

knead → | n | | d |

missed → | m | | t |

not → | k | | t |

6) Unscramble the letters to find a pair of homophones.

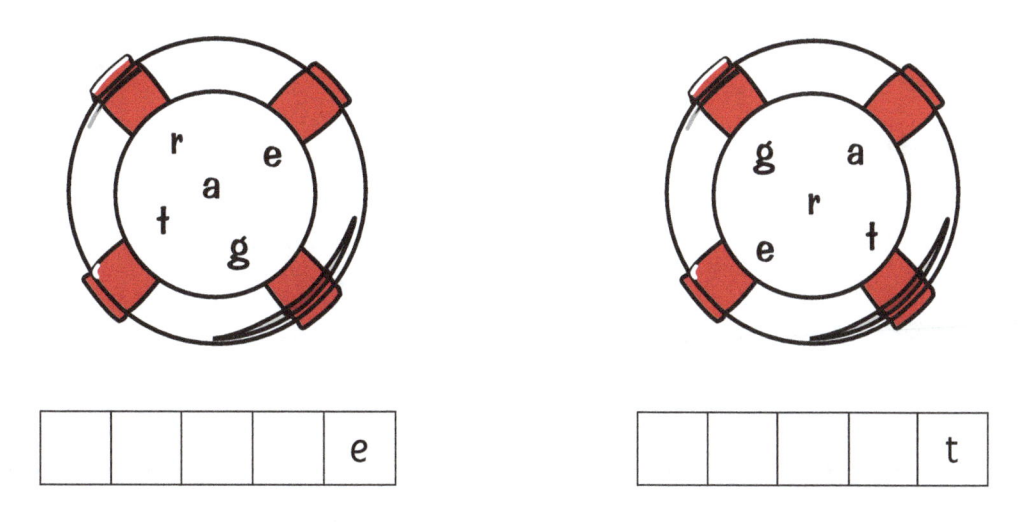

r, e, a, t, g → | | | | | e |

g, a, r, e, t → | | | | | t |

Section 3 — Confusing Words

7 Use one word from each clipboard to make pairs of homophones. Write the pairs on the dotted lines.

Clipboard 1: which, so, tail, stare, new, quay

Clipboard 2: tale, sew, knew, stair, witch, key

Try saying the words out loud to help you do this question.

.... / .... / ....

.... / .... / ....

.... / .... / ....

8 Write each of these words in a sentence.

blue → ....

blew → ....

groan → ....

grown → ....

Now Try This Write a sentence containing the words 'buy', 'bye' and 'by'.

Section 3 — Confusing Words

Spelling Hints and Tips

Spelling can be quite tricky. Here are some hints and tips to help you spell the words that you find most difficult.

1. **Break** the word up into **smaller** parts.
   e.g. al-**pha**-bet   com-**for**-table   hap-**pi**-ness

2. Make up a **sentence** to help you remember how to spell the word.
   e.g. **enough**   **E**lephants **N**ever **O**wn **U**gly **G**rey **H**ats

3. Look for **smaller words** within the word.
   e.g. be**lie**ve   h**ear**d   des**crib**e
   You could make a sentence with both words in to help you remember.
   e.g. Sid the **ant** thinks teamwork is import**ant**.

4. If there's a word that you find **particularly difficult**, try writing it out **correctly** and then **copying** it out lots of times. When you think you know it, try **covering** up the correct spelling and seeing if you can get it right **without looking**.

If you get really stuck, try these tips to help you work out the correct spelling.

1. Remember other words that follow the **same rule**.
   e.g. simple + **ly** = simp**ly**
   gentle + **ly** = gent**ly**

2. Think about words that **sound the same**.
   e.g. hum**orous**   glam**orous**   vig**orous**

3. Think about different ways that **similar sounds** can be spelt.
   e.g. ac**tion**   expre**ssion**   musi**cian**

Spelling Hints and Tips

Answers

Section 1 – Prefixes

Pages 4 and 5 – Prefixes – 'dis' and 'mis'

1. **dis** + **order**
   mis + **lead**
   dis + **own**

2. **mis**print, **mis**shape, **dis**obey, **dis**regard, **mis**treat

3. **dis**advantage
   disbelief
   mishear, **mis**understand
   miscalculated
   disconnect
   mispronounced
   disappointed, **dis**honest

4. **mis**inform
   misjudge
   misspell
   disappear
   disagree

5. **mis**use, **dis**like

Pages 6 and 7 – Prefixes – 'in', 'il', 'im' and 'ir'

1. **in** + **correct**
   il + **legible**
   im + **polite**
   in + **formal**
   in + **direct**
   im + **pure**

2. **im**mortal
   inoffensive
   irreparable
   inadequate

3. **in**capable
   impossible
   irrational
   illogical

4. **in**effective, **ir**regular, **in**valid, **im**proper, **il**legal

5. **im**patient
   inaccurate
   irresistible
   illogical
   irresponsible

Pages 8 and 9 – Prefixes – 're', 'anti' and 'auto'

1. **anti**climax, **re**design, **auto**pilot, **anti**biotic, **re**appear, **re**emerge, **re**open, **anti**septic, **re**fresh

2. **anti**clockwise
   remarried
   autograph
   resend
   antivirus
   rephrase

3. **re**apply
   automobile
   redecorate
   antisocial
   rearrange

4. Fred is writing his **autobiography**.
   I need to **redo** my homework because it got wet.
   Return the form in the envelope provided.
   In winter, people use **antifreeze** spray on their cars.
   Mrs Potter **reheats** her leftover meals in the microwave.

Pages 10 and 11 – Prefixes – 'sub', 'super' and 'inter'

1. **sub**let
   subtotal
   superglue

2. **super**natural, **inter**related, **inter**lock, **super**power, **sub**merge

3. **inter**active
   intercity
   Subheadings
   superglue
   superstar
   superman
   subdivided

Answers

4. **submarine**
   supermarket

5. Any sentence where the word is used correctly.
   Examples:
   I need to think of a **subtitle** for my project.
   If I were a **superhero**, I would be able to turn invisible.
   Ronald booked an **international** flight to Canada.

Section 2 – Suffixes and Word Endings

Pages 12 and 13 – Suffixes – Double Letters

1. You should have ticked: **preferred, offering, equipped**.
   You should have crossed: **prefered, offerring, equiped**.

2. Double letter: swim**ming**, run**ning**, stop**ping**, begin**ning**
   No double letter: jump**ing**, play**ing**, garden**ing**

3. **limited**
   cancelled
   jumped
   singing

4. **beginner**
   gardener
   hotter
   swimmer

5. You should have circled: **traveled, visitted, regreted, poping, feelling**
   The correct spellings are: **travelled, visited, regretted, popping, feeling**

Pages 14 and 15 – Suffixes – 'ation' and 'ous'

1. **donation**
   dangerous
   creation
   expectation
   glamorous

2. You should have underlined: **couragous, humourous, infectous, senseation**.
   The correct spellings are: **courageous, humorous, infectious, sensation**.

3. relax**ation**
   outrage**ous**
   inform**ation**

4. **mountainous**
   humorous
   poisonous

5. You should have circled: **prepareations, celebrateions, inviteations, fameous, locatetion, indicatetions**.
   The correct spellings are: **preparations, celebrations, invitations, famous, location, indications**.

Pages 16 and 17 – Suffixes – 'ly'

1. **sadly, doubly, gladly, subtly, safely, quickly, cuddly**

2. **costly, boldly, calmly, oddly, badly, weakly, softly**

```
H C O S T L Y R O
A S B Q U K H E C
O E O X J E H A
D G L F N O E T L
D T D R T V T E M
L S L I F L I A L
Y M Y V W Z Y H Y
A B A D L Y Q U E
E P W E A K L Y T
```

3. **frantically**
   completely
   gently
   truly
   fiddly
   nobly

4. simple — **simply**
   easy — **easily**
   angry — **angrily**
   happy — **happily**
   dead — **deadly**
   busy — **busily**

Answers

5. Any sentence where the word is used correctly.
   Examples:
   Jason **comically** pulled a funny face.
   Although he was an hour late, Callum **finally** arrived.

Pages 18 and 19 – Word Endings – 'sure' and 'ture'

1. **pressure**, literature, furniture, leisure, torture

2. **enclosure**
   adventure
   mixture
   manufacture
   exposure
   composure
   gesture

3. **treasure**
   picture
   enclosure
   temperature
   signature

4. reas**sure**
   struc**ture**
   mois**ture**
   mea**sure**
   clo**sure**

5. Any words ending in -sure or -ture that are spelt correctly.
   Examples:
   unsure, assure, ensure, insure, closure, pressure
   posture, nurture, vulture, venture, fracture

Pages 20 and 21 – Word Endings – The 'shun' Sound

1. You should have ticked: **permission, division, mention**.
   You should have crossed: **politition, complecian, attencian, hesitacian, musicsion, confesion**.
   The correct spellings are: **politician, completion, attention, hesitation, musician, confession**.

2. **expression, reduction, electrician, direction, discussion, confusion, technician**

3. Across:
   1. **mathematician**
   2. **injection**
   3. **invitation**
   4. **television**
   Down:
   1. **magician**
   2. **invention**

Page 22 – Word Endings – 'gue' and 'que'

1. You should have underlined: **catalog, dialog, intrig**
   The correct spellings are: **catalogue, dialogue, intrigue**

2. anti**que**
   ban**k**
   criti**que**
   drin**k**

3. Any sentence where a word ending in gue or que is used correctly.
   Examples:
   Jean received a **plaque** for winning the competition.
   I felt really tired — I was overcome by **fatigue**.

Section 3 – Confusing Words

Page 23 – Word Families

1. You should have ticked: **sporty, sportsmanship, unsporting**

2. Any correctly spelt words that are in two different word families. Examples:
   disagree, agree**ment**
   replay, play**ful**

3. Any acceptable word that uses the same root.
   Examples:
   thoughtless, writer, uncover

Answers

Page 24 – The Short 'i' Sound

1. You should have circled: **Egypt**, **witch**, **myth**, **gym**

2. You should have ticked: **sympathy**, **satisfy**
   You should have crossed: **sistem**, **rapyd**, **abolysh**, **phisics**
   The correct spellings are: **system**, **rapid**, **abolish**, **physics**

3. **mistakes**
   symbols

Page 25 – The Short 'u' Sound

1. **u**mbrella, t**ou**ch

2. **double**
   nothing
   Rough
   brother
   cousin

3. Any sentence where the word is used correctly.
   Examples:
   Spain is a **country** in Europe.
   He looks too **young** to be at university.
   There isn't **enough** for everyone.

Page 26 – The Hard 'c' Sound

1. **leak**, **chord**, **brick**, **smoke**, **electric**

2. **ch**aos, awa**k**e, **ch**emist, an**ch**or, **ch**aracter, **k**ettle, tri**ck**, **c**are, e**ch**o, sti**ck**

3. **mechanic**
   chorus
   calendar
   soccer

Page 27 – The Soft 'c' Sound

1. **pace**, **science**, **recipe**, **crescent**

2. You should have underlined: **prinsce**, **parcel**, **deside**, **decend**, **suspence**
   The correct spellings are: **prince**, **parcel**, **decide**, **descend**, **suspense**

3. Any sentence where the word is used correctly.
   Examples:
   Discipline and restraint are good qualities.
   The special effects **fascinate** me.
   There was a very strange **scent** in the air.
   Let me set the **scene** for you.

Page 28 – The 'sh' Sound

1. wi**sh**, poli**sh**, **ch**arade, radi**sh**, **ch**ivalry, pre**ss**ure, **sh**immer, **sh**adow, para**ch**ute

2. **ch**ef
   bro**ch**ure
   sure
   ma**ch**ine
   pari**sh**

3. Any sentence where the word is used correctly.
   Examples:
   I need to **insure** my new car.
   He has committed a crime and we must **punish** him.
   I think my dad's **moustache** is impressive.

Page 29 – The 'ay' Sound

1. You should have circled: **obay**, **veighl**, **neibour**, **shaike**
   The correct spellings are: **obey**, **veil** or **vale**, **neighbour**, **shake**

2. **afraid**
   freight
   hesitate

3. **plain**, **eight**

Pages 30 and 31 – Plurals and Apostrophes

1. You should have ticked:
   The witches' cauldrons
   The women's handbags

2. men**'s**, deer**'s**, beaches**'**, cats**'**

Answers

Answers

3. You should have underlined:
   the elves' hats
   the ladies' coats
   the boxes' labels
   the calves' mothers
   the policemen's handcuffs
   the companies' employees

4. **the students' books**
   the children's toys
   the snowmen's scarves

5. More than one shoe belonging to more than one girl — **The girls' shoes**
   One shoe belonging to one girl — **The girl's shoe**
   One shoe belonging to more than one girl — **The girls' shoe**

6. Any sentence that uses possessive apostrophes correctly.
   Examples:
   The mice**'s** mother watched carefully for the cat.
   Snakes**'** tongues are very long.
   The geese**'s** wings helped them to fly.

Pages 32 to 34 – Homophones

1. You should have matched:
   piece with "part of something"
   peace with "calm and quiet"
   plain with "simple or ordinary"
   plane with "a flying vehicle"

2. **aisle**
   Isle
   I'll

3. You should have circled: **ate**, **air**, **dear**
   The correct spellings are: **eight**, **heir**, **deer**

4. **He'll** definitely be late.
   Shoes that don't fit properly often rub on the **heel**.
   I hope my injury will **heal** soon.

5. **seen**, **fair**, **flea**, **need**, **mist**, **knot**

6. **grate**, **great**

7. **which** / **witch**
   so / **sew**
   tail / **tale**
   stare / **stair**
   new / **knew**
   quay / **key**

8. Any sentence where the word is used correctly.
   Examples:
   Blue is my favourite colour.
   I **blew** the whistle to end the game.
   Jim heard a loud **groan**.
   You can buy expensive clothes when you are fully **grown**.